Gardens of the Sisterhood

Create a Mystical–Healing Garden

Ann Marie O'Dell

BALBOA.PRESS
A DIVISION OF HAY HOUSE

Balboa Press books may be ordered through booksellers or by contacting:

Balboa Press
A Division of Hay House
1663 Liberty Drive
Bloomington, IN 47403
www.balboapress.com
1 (877) 407-4847

ISBN: 978-1-9822-4270-1 (sc)
ISBN: 978-1-9822-4271-8 (e)

Print information available on the last page.

Balboa Press rev. date: 02/19/2020

Feminine Wisdom and Creativity

A WOMAN'S GARDEN VISION IS A SPIRITUAL
JOURNEY OF HER OWN CREATION.

Gardens of the Sisterhood

CREATE A MYSTICAL-HEALING GARDEN
BY ANN MARIE O'DELL

We can heal ourselves and heal our world through the creation of a Mystical Garden. Embrace Spirituality, mass intention, and thought principles through your garden. With the Mystical-Healing support of Sisterhood, tune in and live in the moment, and join the movement to slow civilization's frantic pace of action. Humanity seems headed towards self-destruction. It's time to review the Ancient Principles of Cause and Effect, and how indifference to energy fields around us can create disaster instead of healing. Create a dramatic entrance to your shop or home and blend with your community as an Alternative Worker.

Contents

Alternative Healing & Intuition

The Importance of BLENDING with COMMUNITY and EARTH

Intuition, Clairvoyance, Empathy

THE IMPORTANCE OF BLENDING AS AN ALTERNATIVE HEALER

I am one of the new breed of Spiritual Advisers, who no longer have to work from a metropolitan city shop. Living in a small town perched on blacktop America, I can read for clients by phone and Email nationally and abroad. Intuition, Clairvoyance, and Empathy are not regional, but a human experience. Healing is not just for religious Masters, and Alternative Workers who gain an esteemed reputation for their skills. For this reason, it has never been more important to learn how to blend in as a respected community member. Designing your home or shop entrance in sync with compatible neighborhood essence will allow you to be accepted in peace.

The Entrance

GARDEN PORTALS

The secret to a wonderful shop or garden is the entrance, and the ability to be successful in a conservative town is not by banners of Third Eye or a neon sign announcing "PSYCHIC," or "MASSAGE." The key to staying in business is gaining the trust of the neighbors/store keepers around you. Even if they do not agree with your belief system, helpful consideration will make you friends. Boundaries and meticulous upkeep of a shop are extremely important while maintaining a profile of integrity. What you do for a living will usually be accepted.

My journey
Frequencies and Essence
Reading the Historical Land Energy of Your Garden

Each garden has its historical imprint. Shake hands with the historical spirit of your garden before plunging a shovel into its mantle. Know that the elements of the past will affect you. Parallel worlds run beside the present. As you sit in your artistic garden chair, choose the frequency of the land carefully before creating a space to sip tea, or share wine. Bond with the elements of the earth with Divination tools. Ask these questions:

With Tarot, Runes, Automatic Writing or a Pendulum Ask:

- "What essence lives here?"
- "What is the frequency of this place?"
- "What does earth-spirit wish me to know?"
- "How can we work together?"

Be prepared to hear reluctance for your changes. Forcing your will on angry land can lead to dying gardens, a feeling of anxiety and dread, and haunted dwellings. Choose to plant or create a relaxing pathway, drum circle or Sisterhood ceremony on land that welcomes you.

My Intuitive Experience

FROM PACKING HOUSE WORK TO AN ANGEL MESSENGER

At 19 I discovered Tarot cards in a French gift shop and quickly learned to read them with great accuracy at coffee houses and art fairs. Aware that I was leaving my chapter as a single Mom behind on my son's graduation, staying with a packing house job I saw as survival since he was four years old, seemed ridiculous. Instead, I spread my wings to become a full-time reader. One blessing led to another. Soon the little house across the lane from me went up for sale and became my studio. As if in a trance, I found myself reading the land intuitively, placing gardens on the ground with good energy. I took my analytical mind out of the process and certified in Transpersonal Hypnotherapy and Reiki, wrote books, became a Spiritual Radio Host and joined a Sisterhood.

Follow the voice of your Intuitive Guidance. Amazing things can happen.

Slow Down in a Fast-Paced World

What is a Healing Garden?

As the world goes faster and faster, and we are lost in the existence of technology, schedules, competition, and mandates, slowing down and relaxing takes as much discipline as daily Meditation and Exercise. We need a Healing Garden to slow down and savor the minutes. As women of unlimited leadership in crisis, matriarchs of our families and communities, we teach, heal and influence through example.

We consume vitamins and smoothies and purified water in an attempt to live longer and be more healthy while self-sabotaging ourselves in an ever-present state of chronic stress. Sleep becomes impossible. We are haunted by never-ending "what-ifs."

For women, it can be chronic yeast infections, inability to conceive a child, and increases in the risk of heart attack and stroke. We need a supportive Sisterhood to back us when times get rough.

THE SLOW MOVEMENT

Slowing down our movements is a movement toward slowing down one's life pace. What it is not, is to do everything in slow motion.

- Slow living is timeless and based on ancient wisdom and spirituality, much of which is found in the Principles of Feng Shui and Druid Gardening.
- Slow living is about pacing your actions and plans in a steady and consistent manner.
- Slow living is taking the analytical mind out of every minute and Spiritually savoring moments spent reading, bonding, and exercising instead of running ten steps ahead of ourselves.

Angel Healing

Bless Your Plants and Pets with Healing Energy

LISTENING HANDS

Each of us holds unlimited energetic healing ability. As children, we are taught to see this as only the gift of Masters. In Reiki, the healing ability passes from master to student through attunements. The energetic ability to move a spiral of healing from our hands to plants, humans, and animals, is also defined as "listening hands ." Students trained to pay attention to the feel of subtle energetic shifts in their hands, such as tingling, changes of hot and cold, visualize light and energy pouring from above, into their hands, transferring healing into what or who they touch. For those who are transcending into death, "Listening Hands" can soothe and balance Hospice patients.

- Find a time of day to give your sick Pet or plants attention
- Imagine a healing spiral in your hands, rotating around and around
- Feel your hands heat up, empowered with energy
- Now hold your hands close to your plants
- Focus on the spirals in your palms filled with light as you hold them above your plants, pets, or yourself.

ALTERNATIVE HEALING IN CONSERVATIVE COMMUNITIES

Have names and numbers of traditional healers in the community. As a Certified Holistic Practitioner or Intuitive Advisor, you will find more open-mindedness towards what you do, by who you know. By working compatibly, rather than condemning what is different than you, you'll become an accepted Partner. If you have done all you can, and a client's problems are more profound than your expertise, take the weight off your shoulders. Empowerment is admitting when something is over your head. Direct a client to more qualified sources.

How Do You Think?

Do You Think In Circular Patterns?

FREE SPIRIT

You are a free spirit, heeding the call of nature. Mystical Healing Gardens, designed with intriguing circular paths, embrace the spiral and the DNA code of Mother Earth. Circles are connected to the movement, heart, and womb of the natural world. In a sort of stem cell reboot, Circles and Spirals energetically amplify and enhance the healing process.

Designing Your Garden In Circles

- When used as a background pattern, Circles create a sense of flow and calmness. They bring focus to sculpture, an ornamental tree, or a garden mirror.
- A perfect shape, a spiral, triggers powerful healing, emotionally, and physically, and clears the mind.
- A teepee makes an amazing circular garden for climbing vines
- An herb spiral makes a stand out circular garden
- Place a bench in the center of a circular garden for an inviting place to sit.

Types of Circular Gardens

- **Native American Medicine Wheel** - Sacred symbol used by Plains tribes and others representing all knowledge of the universe.
- **Circular Labyrinth** – An ancient symbol that combines the imagery of the circle and the spiral of truth representing a journey to our own center.
- **Circular Medicinal Herb Garden –** Magic and Healing Herbs.
- **Spiral Garden – The Druid Garden –** Spirals can be found in paintings in caves and carved in stones as far back as 8000 BCE and represents the life force cycle of life.
- **Circular Celtic Knot Garden** - represents eternity of loyalty, faith, and love.

Do You Think In Right Angles?

The Strategist

DO YOU THINK IN SQUARES?

Do you find yourself placing everything in right angles? You are a leader in your home that needs to mark your identity, and create order and discipline. Put you in charge of an art display or flea market, and you will quickly convert displays into squares. Squares are historically the center of communities and cities.

A great city square has a variety of smaller "places" within it to appeal to the needs of people. Ten places, each with ten things to do, offers a full program for a successful festival, healing garden and city. These might include outdoor tables, water fountains, sculptures, and even a makeshift performance stage or Gazebo for weddings or performances.

In your garden, a bench in just the right location, Artwork, sculpture or water feature can be magnets for visitors and your morning walks with coffee. Think of social interaction or a tribal Sisterhood gathering.

TYPES OF SQUARE GARDENS

The square's popularity is most used for gardens due to its ease of equal watering, fertilizing, and easy access to rows of plants.

- Traditional Vegetable Garden
- Japanese Moss Garden
- City Squares
- Rose Gardens
- Raised Bed Gardening
- Square Foot Gardening

Practical Shamanism

ADAPTING TO COMMUNITY NEEDS

ALTERNATIVE HEALING – Contemporary Shamanism

When all traditional healing has been tried for emotional or physical trauma, and conventional approaches are not working, the next step for many is to consult a Shaman. From Buddhism to Christianity, ancient shamanic roots bear threads of deep connection to the Divine in all things.

Shamans were the first physicians and psychotherapists. Found in cultures all over the world, Shamanism is practical healing, adapting to the needs of the community it serves. Its core belief is that all illness has an underlying Spiritual or Energetic issue that needs addressing for there to be true healing.

Today, shamanism is studied and practiced as a life path. Much in the way that prayer from a minister or priest acts as a way to speak to God, the Shaman, going into a deep meditative state, turns the needs of their seeker, through means of consulting the Divine, into manifested reality.

Contemporary western shamanism bears little resemblance to old traditions, and often a Shaman may also be a Reiki Master or Ortho-Bionomy Practitioner. As an adaptable and practical spiritual healing modality, with deep roots into the Divine, people are finding their way to contemporary shamans for the health conditions which traditional medicine cannot resolve.

Drum Circles

RHYTHM OF THE GARDEN PATH

What happens when you are energy depleted? Pack your hand-painted medicine drum, rain sticks, and gypsy shawl in the car and find a drum circle. Better yet, host one. If you want to be the facilitator of a drum circle, be sure to prepare the space well ahead of time before the guests arrive.

WHAT IS A DRUM CIRCLE?

A drum circle can range from just a few players or an entire city block of participants. Sitting in a circle, people play hand-drums and percussion, The beauty of a drum circle is it is casual, and not at all prepared performance. You can choose to leave early or stay until the wee hours.

FACILITATOR OF A DRUM CIRCLE

If you are the chosen leader of the drum circle, prepare your event ahead of time. With your unique touches, make your space welcoming. Take into consideration there may be dancers and give plenty of space for an audience. A comfortable place for your drum circle, in winter, would be the basement of the Unitarian Church or a park shelter with a fireplace with easy parking access. Add water, refreshments, and food. In the summer take your Sisterhood into the Healing Garden, and inhale the aroma of a Moon Garden.

DON'T FORGET TO DANCE

For those who would rather dance, here is where your shawl comes in. Wrap it around your shoulders or down by your hips. You can stand in one place, shuffle, do a simple two-step or leap to the rhythm. Your participation, no matter how small, will make the event magical.

The Angel Frequency

POSITIVE THINKING THROUGH THE STORMS OF LIFE

SHELTER, CONTRIBUTE, REINFORCE

There are gates to Angelic dimensions. Sometimes a dream offers you the key to unlock the answers to your next life stage. The healing that awaits you inside, changes the way you see the world. A life crisis can give strength, and in the history of man has led to evolution. In the history of human life, it's the path to personal transformation.

Beneath your feet in the living world, you go deeper towards your destiny. Destruction can be right around the corner. Choosing to live in the Angel Frequency, you tend to your own and what is before you. You shelter, contribute, reinforce, diminish chaos, and establish order with love. You brave new realities and become an example. As you walk through spiritual dimensions, fearlessly, your intuition soars and guides the way.

Rainbow Healing

Chakra Reflections

Each of the colors of the rainbow reflects from a Prism in the Sunlight. You bask in the magical colors bouncing on the wall as your prism twirls on a chain in front of your window. Red - family. Orange- stomach. Gold - Solar Plexus. Green and Pink - Heart. Blue - Throat chakra. Purple - third eye. White - Crown. A feeling of childlike joy floods into you all the while you are immersed in a Natural Reiki Rainbow Healing session.

For continuous rainbows choose a bright sunny South window to hang your crystals. Swarovski Crystals will deliver the best rainbows and explode in reflective, highly intense colors. Plastic Prisms are pretty but do not reflect light effectively. Choose Swarovski Crystals to hang in windows. For the pleasure of older children, running their fingers through a bowl of smooth colored prisms with the consistency of garden stones is a safe and magical pleasure. Create mobiles from high-quality Swarovski prisms and watch healing pathways come alive with Reiki Rainbow Healing.

Creating the Healing Garden

STRUCTURE, PATHWAYS, ENERGY OF THE MYSTICAL HEALING GARDEN

Soul Palette Colors

FLOWER COLORS IN THE GARDEN

1) BLUE, the color of the Throat Chakra, has a pacifying effect on the nervous system. Choose neutral and soft blue flowers for a relaxing sitting space to slow down the heart rate. To represent Wisdom and enhance communication and speech, a neutral and soft blue will create an excellent conduit for Sisterhood circles with problem-solving journey work. Are you a blue personality? Loyalty, Trust, Tactful Diplomacy, and Calm people are drawn to the color blue.

2) GREEN, the Fourth chakra of Love and Self-love, relaxes stressful thoughts and muscles, and reminds us of the importance of giving and taking unconditionally. Mystical Healing Gardens with mass plantings of abundant green ferns and hosta offer a rich tapestry of shape, texture, and a serene haven from the sun. People who love green have the personality traits of understanding, self-control, adaptability, sympathy, compassion, generosity, humbleness, and are nature-loving and romantic.

3) PINK is the color of friendship, affection, harmony, and inner peace. In the Mystical Healing Garden, pink will smooth agitated thoughts, especially concerning romantic and family relationship worries. Add pink to your Mystical Healing Garden to add innocence and warmth. Those with a soul connection with pink are generally gentle, casual, and approachable.

4) WHITE, the Seventh Crown Chakra, is pure and symbolizes oneness in the universe. In images of the ascended masters, the activated Crown chakra can appear like a halo. In the Mystical Healing Garden, the color white can create the essence of enlightenment, like the light from a lantern, bouncing here and there on the pathway ahead. White symbolizes clarity and freshness, and in times of stress it is the right color to gain clarity in your thoughts.

5) VIOLET is the Sixth Chakra of the Third Eye. Violet signifies strength, peace, and wisdom, giving Balance to the Mystical Garden. Said to increase bone growth the color violet brings a balance of potassium and sodium within the body. If meditation is your intent, the power of inner focus can be ten times greater under violet light. For Intuitive Reading, add a violet or purple grow light in your space to add clarity and enhanced psychic ability. For wisdom and insight in the Mystical Healing Garden, add violet or purple flowers for drama, spirituality, psychic awareness, higher self, and passion.

6) SILVER - GREY symbolizes Reflection and Changes in Direction. A soothing and cooling presence when paired with blue or white elements in the Mystical Healing Garden, it energizes during the new and full moons. Silver-grey adds emotional dignity, self-control, wisdom, responsibility, organization, and insight for overwhelming stress. When worn, Silver draws negative energy from the body, replacing it with positive energy. Look for this color to add neutrality within the Mystical Healing Garden.

7) YELLOW is the Third Chakra, the Solar Plexus. Yellow's golden essence, associated with the sun and high volumes of energy, brings a sense of joy and confidence in the body. In the Mystical Healing Garden, yellow marigolds or other yellow blossoms aid in giving insight, hope, and courage to thoughts on a new job, living relocation, or seeing the positive benefits of divorce, parenthood, or empty nest syndrome.

Maiden, Mother, Crone

SPIRITUAL GARDENS OF THE SISTERHOOD

The preparation and planting of the seed into fertile soil, bringing forth the new sprout, represents the Maiden. The fresh, beautiful bloom as it opens its dewy stamen in pollination represents the Mother. The harvest represents the Crone or Wise Woman and is the wisdom that comes from an abundant life journey. Spiritual Gardens have roots as deep as the domestication of land beginning with the Hanging Gardens of Babylon and places of the ancient spiritual ceremonies by Sisters of Mesopotamia and Pompeii.

The Journey of the Maiden - a Contemporary Journey

In the old days, girls were gifted with dolls and toy kitchen appliances to prepare them for the journey of being a mother and wife. It is more common now to see little girls wearing fairy costumes, as they take on the attitude that they can become whatever they want. Magical. Encouraged to be scientists, oceanographers, and to have an earth mission is more the norm as little girls are encouraged to be empowered.

By the time little girls have turned into adolescents, the concept of being empowered can be confusing. Where relationships were number one in the eyes of all young women, the internet offers love through the eyes of mass cyber world. The problem with this is bullying in a grand scale. With the addition of birth control, unexpected pregnancy is not the fear as much as an STD from unprotected sex. She is still the beautiful Maiden on a Unicorn, galloping her way to a University, World Travel, and Adventure.

The Journey of the Mother

As a single mother, I was the breadwinner and nurturer, with no desire to have more than one child as life was expensive. I was a realist of what I could and could not do, but also an artist who performed on stage and read cards and palms in the local coffee house. If I could not create I was depressed and the addition of hormones made mood swings horrific.

There were dreams I flushed down the toilet in order to be what my mother of four girls taught me through example. She worked outside the home, came home, cooked dinner for her daughters, paid the bills and gardened. It was my example of what a good mother does. But my mother always had a man. I too, good or bad, have always had a relationship. Then comes the torture of many single Moms. How does the lover or partner treat my child? How does my child feel about the partner I have brought into our lives? How will my own image in my child's eyes be affected? With one child, I experienced empty nest syndrome at the age of forty as he flew off to Japan to join the Navy. Desertion. Now what? A line of single parents sobbed, like me, as our sons and daughters flew away on a plane to Asia.

The Journey of the Crone

The in-between years of forty and fifty years old were a mixture of perimenopause, hormone replacement, and second adolescence. As I smoothly avoided Menopause with "Premarin," at one time called the miracle drug for movie stars, my skin glowed, I was vivacious, sexual, taut, and I loved me so much! I noticed I was being approached and followed by men much younger than myself. It was then I discovered, like most women, I was throwing out the last of my baby-making pheromones equivalent to an eighteen-year-old male. This crashed to a halt completely like a semi-truck throwing on the breaks. Full Menopause hit.

I became invisible!

Without the pheromones, which act as a silent baby-making call to men, I was a blank slate. I found that the second glances, secret smiles, and heads up as I walked into a room stopped. This meant, surprisingly, I was no longer competition for other women, and they magically became more friendly. Hello Sisterhood, where have you been all my life? (I loved you, but you acted intimidated.) I was amazed how in my struggle to appear flawless, a few wrinkles, sags, and extra weight made me less a threat! Or maybe I became more humble.

A beautiful thing happened when I turned fifty. I found myself filled with peace as the insanity of hormones were gone! My childhood gift of intuition soared like a bird. I got married. And the beauty of a blossoming Sisterhood, a tribal member of feminine empowerment, had nothing to do with a perfect body or looking twenty years old. Good health, good food, and exercise became mainstays. Best of all, the essence of the childhood me came back.

Like many grandmothers, my son and his wife moved far away to find their own journey. The relationship with my two grandchildren has suffered, and I am an invisible grandmother. I cried, but now accept, and find solace in my creativity and Sisterhood. I am like many grandmothers who will not be a matriarch figurehead in their grandchildren's lives in sorrow. We can travel to see them, but it's not the same as being close. We miss out on their changes.

It becomes essential to slow down, to get out of my head, savor the moments I am in control of making for myself. Choosing joy, creativity, travel when able, instead of harboring hostility and self-pity of what I can not control. This is the wisdom of the Crone.

Fabric and Garden Arches

CHOOSING FLOWING FABRICS

There is nothing more lovely than a beautiful scarf or fabric billowing in the wind on an Arch or Arbor. As morning sunlight shines through the fabric, it shimmers like a jewel. Fabric wrapped arches are not just for weddings. Many believe that cloth is too delicate to stand up to wind and rain. Choosing a flowing fabric that is sturdy enough to endure summer storms and to dry quickly is important. Choosing the right fabric, and wrapping or tacking it well, will provide summer-long color and movement.

Decide how much light you want to shine through your fabric then choose from these three categories: Translucent, Sheer, Opaque

The Six Most "Billowy" Fabrics for Your Garden Arch

- Satin – Opaque
- Cotton Voile – Sheer
- Charmeuse – Opaque, Drapes well,
- Chiffon – Sheer and Gauzy
- Gossamer – Semi Sheer, Translucent, Gauzy
- Tulle – Transparent, Sturdy Outdoor All Summer Long Fabric

Techniques for Draping and Attaching

- Wrapped
- Hung
- Drooped
- Puddled

Fabric Dream Catchers in the Iris

EMBROIDERY HOOPS AND FABRIC – JOY IN THE GARDEN

A famed Tennessee Mountain grower who specialized in acres of Rainbow Hued Iris passed away. What was to become of her show-stopping gardens? Quickly the local Garden Clubs stepped in! With shovels, pickups, knee pads, and wheelbarrows the women rescued the flowers from the yard before the land transferred to a person with no interest in Iris.

A woman's garden vision is a spiritual journey of her own creation.

As Kate watched her new amazing 1000 Rainbow Iris grow, taking on the vision of a Sisterhood Matriarch before her, she fell in love with her chickens, herbs, and nodding bearded flower heads as if living in a dream. It was then she ran to the store and purchased different sizes of wood embroidery hoops. Browsing the local fabric store for remnants of brilliant colors of cloth and lace, she bought an entire cloth bag full. Once home, in a blaze of passion, she ripped and cut strips of the fabric and tied them around the circumference of fifteen wood hoops of various sizes. The effect was dazzling as she hung her Dream Catchers above the Iris, tails of ribbon, lace, and fabric blowing in the wind. It was a Stop The Car vision for all to share as the vision of a Sister became her own.

Kinetic Wind Sculptures

FLOW AND MOVEMENT WITHIN THE HEALING GARDEN

Kinetic Wind Sculptures add an other-worldly art spectrum to the flow of the land. They can be spectacular or simple, and offer a hypnotic, meditative quality to those that gaze in a trance as the movable sculpture spins in a flowing marriage with the wind.

Spiritual Wind Chimes

WIND MUSIC WITHIN THE HEALING GARDEN

Just as you would not want to listen to an out of tune band or a voice that can not hit the right notes, your wind chimes should sing in a melodic and harmonizing song. Wood and Ocean Shells have soothing tones together. When choosing multiple metal windchimes, pick professionally tuned chimes designed to blow in the wind in harmony.

Creating a Garden Pathway
THE BONES OF THE GARDEN

The pathway through a garden can be unaffordable and organic, or sophisticated and creative. When the garden path is in order and clutter-free, we feel the benefits of an unobstructed flow of energy called "Chi." Just as the arteries in our body respond to clean eating, the energy called "Chi" will bless our lives with good health and clear thinking.

ARTFUL PATHWAYS

When considering your pathway take into consideration that you will want it wide enough to roll a wheelbarrow filled with your garden supplies on, as well as have a comfortable walk for two. For this reason, the more you use your path the wider it should be. A minimum of four feet wide is best, and to accommodate disabilities, 5 feet wide.

THE PATH SUBSTANCE

Choose Pea rock, crushed gravel or crushed limestone, to make long-lasting pathways that need only occasional weeding. Crushed shells or stone make beautiful pathways.

PATH EDGING

When placing an outside border on the sides of your path, make it 4 inches wide and 2 inches deep to separate flower beds or grass.

PATH NETWORK

Proportionally, a narrow garden needs a narrow pathway. Your garden will appear wider creating a path from one side across to the other. Vertical plant towers will draw the eyes upward.

REST STOPS OF THE PATHWAY

Working in your garden, observing plant growth and the birds, a place to sit will be a welcome addition on the path. Choose a beautiful bench, a large rock, or a tree stump to sit on. Like the dinner table you will soon be sitting on your favorite spot every time you are outside.

Statuary in the Healing Garden
EXPRESSING YOUR ESSENCE AND LIFE JOURNEY

The style of your garden should be matched by the statues and sculptures placed in it. Before choosing a statue ask yourself:

- What is the style of my garden? Will large slabs of Stone or Sculpture fit the aesthetics?
- Consider the directional energy and whether your statuary will blend.
- Where is the best view in your garden for a statue to be seen?
- Why does a statue or organic element stand out to you? What does it mean to you and express to visitors or clients?
- Will you need a Pedestal or will it be directly on the ground?

What Is An Eclectic Garden?

I SHARE MY SOUL THROUGH THE GARDEN

An Eclectic Garden combines the ideas and influences absorbed through the gardener's lifetime, their fascinations, travel, studies, and wisdom. Often one garden theme leads to another. This is not the same as a whimsical garden of Innerchild, but of concepts and philosophies.

For instance, a formal garden hedge expressing the love of castles may lead to a bright sunny cottage garden with an explosion of poppies and other colorful flowers. As you walk around the house, the energy changes. Suddenly you are in the cool shade of a massive tree, surrounded by Hostas and the deep sound of melodic chimes. Even the birds seem to sing differently, matching the calm of the back yard. As you walk into the house, you have subconsciously absorbed all the exciting facets of the person you are visiting.

TYPES OF THEME GARDENS

@ Asian Gardens

@ Cottage Gardens

@ Prairie Flower Gardens

@ Woodland Gardens

@ Formal Gardens

@ Water Gardens

@ Shade Gardens

What is a Moon Garden?

LUMINOUS WHITE, FRAGRANCE IN THE NIGHT

My love for Moon Gardens began on a backroad ride with my dogs. I was in awe of a simple square white farmhouse, its backdoor cement steps leading to a set of old wicker chairs positioned at the base of a five-foot retaining wall.

The ground at the top of the retaining wall, bordered with tall white rods of phlox, was planted with white Petunia. Cascading like a frothing waterfall towards the ground, the wave of white Petunia met a thick fluffy carpet of white Impatiens and Alyssum, which carried the momentum forward to encircle two nearby maple trees and the circle of cement where the chairs resided.

The finished look was stunning and Angelic. I loved seeing the couple sitting in clouds of white flowers, drinking their evening coffee. The fragrance must-have been wonderful. By the end of summer, I was a frequent sight as they waved at me as I passed by.

There are Four Types of flowers used in moon gardens:

- Plants with white flowers
- Plants with bright foliage
- Night bloomers
- Plants with fragrant blooms

The use of mass color can have a dramatic visual impact in your landscape. Mass planting is especially important in a nighttime moon garden. Beneath a luminous night sky, the flowers glow with a mystical other-worldly beauty. Within the white flowers, a few solar lights, just enough to enhance, will empower the vision.

Keep the white flowers coming in a Seasonal moonlit display by planting early bloomers early-to-mid spring. By mid-summer, many Perennials leave the landscape. Fill empty spaces with white annuals. Autumn will take over with white Phlox. Don't forget the spectacular display that silver and white Hosta can also contribute.

A Druid's Garden –

THE THREE SACRED ELEMENTS

THE PHILOSOPHICAL HYPOTHESIS & SCIENCE
OF THE MYSTICAL HEALING GARDEN

Druids were a combination of Community Advisor, Teacher, Philosopher, Scientist, and Judge. Though not priests, they were the diplomatic connection between man and the Gods. They preferred Oral teaching over writing, so there is little known about them other than what is passed down from one man to another through history. Scholars of the natural world, they considered trees as sacred and saw the world based around Three Elements. These concepts are the headstone of the Contemporary Druid Garden .

THE THREE DRUID ELEMENTS: Nwyfre, Calas, and Gwyar

Nwyfre (NOOiv-ruh),The first Druid Element represents the energy of the garden, its life force and consciousness associated with the sky and heavens. In the garden, it is the spiritual energy of the plant, and the unseen spaces between all living things.

Gwyar (GOO-yar), The Second Druid Element represents the flow, movement, and change of living things seen and unseen. The conversion of light into energy would be an example of how, through the process of photosynthesis, plants eat sunlight and carbon dioxide to produce their food. The blood in our veins that flows to our organs, allowing energy and health would be the element of Gwyar. The orchestration of flow and movement in the process of decay, whereby the earth, fertilized, stimulates the production of microbes in a complete circle.

Calas (CAH-lass) The Third Druid Element is the finished product, healing properties of what happens when the energy and light, flow and movement, create the carrot on our plate. Whatever is the conclusion as a result of the first and second property.

Contemporary Druid Philosophy contains the basic elements of Hypotheses for all life questions and spirit. It is the contemplation and strategy behind science and theory.

The Whimsical Garden
THE PORTAL OF INNER CHILD

Curiouser and Curiouser is the theme of a Whimsical garden. Think of Alice in Wonderland, reflective mirrors, fairy tales and the magical wonder of a child. But be careful, there must be a balance! The nucleus of a Whimsical Garden is a single color that winds like a silk thread through contained chaos, giving stability and balance to all. Whimsey is fun, light-hearted, and folk art-based. It can be a ceramic pot turned on its side with flowers spilling out like milk.

MAINTAINING BALANCE IN THE WHIMSICAL GARDEN

A beautiful childhood is full of wonder and playfulness, with room to spend hours in imagination. But be cautious of overwhelming the six senses. Too much visibility creates invisibility. There needs to be a sense of exploration and suspense in the garden. What lies around the corner to be discovered? Balance in a Whimsical Garden is filled with unexpected surprises.

- Create hiding spots to view the garden unseen by others
- Place a Mirror in an unexpected cool nook, safely wired against a trellis, protected from storms. Alice In Wonderland began her journey by seeing the world in reverse through the looking glass.
- Place a whimsical table and two chairs, painted bright colors, to share a conversation or a cup of coffee with a friend at the end of a path.
- Hang prisms or tiny mirrors from the twisted limbs of a Harry Lauder's Walking Stick shrub. Rainbows and prisms will reflect in the most unexpected places like tiny fairies.

Cannabis In The Healing Garden

For Centuries Marijuana Plants were used as 'Companions' for Garden Vegetables

With the legalization of Cannabis comes the ability to bring relief from pain, anxiety, and insomnia. For Terminal illness, it eliminates much of the need for pharmaceutical Opiates. With the legalization of the beautiful light green herb, it can be planted in a raised bed among the vegetables and be as easy to reach for as Basil for a seasoning herb for cooking. In much the same way winemakers grow grapes on archways, Cannabis in the healing garden will be accessible for texture, color, and healing for common human conditions.

Cannabis is one of the very few plants that create male and female plants, with the female plant producing lush, voluptuous buds that contain the healing components that cure insomnia and anxiety. In the Cannabis Healing Garden, the budding female plants are the focus. Male Cannabis has a shorter life span than the female plant. The male plants are tall, spindly, budless, and hold no cerebral properties. Their thick hollow stems are best for making fiber. Its healing properties are in its fragrant leaves, which can be used in healthy juices. However, the male plants, like male drone bees whose primary function is to fertilize the Queen, are necessary to assure suitable mates for the female plants.

WHAT NO ONE TOLD US ABOUT OUR NATURAL CANNABINOID SYSTEM

The human body has a natural endocannabinoid system called ECS, which in our biological system is composed of lipid-based neurotransmitters. Throughout the vertebrate central nervous system, including the brain, our natural ECS is involved in the cognitive processes, fertility, pregnancy, and during pre and postnatal development. Our natural cannabinoid transmitter proteins also influence appetite, pain sensation, mood, and memory as well as meditation.

Perhaps this is why our Ancestors, Native Americans, and Indigenous tribes have long embraced Cannabis for healing and Spiritual enhancement.

The Garden Bench

AESTHETICS OR FUNCTION?

THE REST STOP OF A GARDEN DESTINATION

Garden Benches are like highway rest stops between destinations. Place them by the most used entry of the house, or on a pathway of heavy foot traffic. Often a bench seats two and should be long enough to accommodate two good-sized men.

Benches With Purpose

- Benches with built-in backs will allow you to sit upright more comfortably.
- Layer the bench with soft cushions for color and comfort.
- Benches without arms will be appreciated by musicians who do not want to bump expensive instruments while entertaining.
- For the elderly or physically disabled, choose sturdy wooden benches with solid arms to hold on to for getting up and down.

BEST PLACES TO PLACE A BENCH

NORTH: Direction of Business, Career, Life Purpose

BENCH: Place a bench along the path for clients to rest,

WATER: Place a small water fountain next to the bench

FLOWERS: Blue, Black

SOUTH : Direction of Recognition, Fame, Entertainment

BENCH: A Gazebo, Long Benches for observing the flowers, nature, entertaining

FIRE: Place your fire pit close to entertainment benches

FLOWERS: Shades of Red

EAST: Direction of Family, Health,

BENCH: Comfie wood benches, Tree Stumps, Wood Deck

WOOD: The treehouse, picnic table, studio/She-Shack

FLOWERS: Green, Brown

WEST: Descendants, Children, Creativity, Mystery

BENCH: Sturdy ample seating for Reunions, gatherings of artist guilds, music jams, poets,

METAL: Traditional iron benches, clusters of benches

FLOWERS: Silver, White, Gold

Bird Aviaries for the Healing Garden

The Sound of Happy Birds
Brings Joy to our Souls

INDOOR BIRD AVIARIES

A Bird Aviary can be a Healing and Calming oasis for bird-lovers who want a sizeable compassionate enclosure that enables flight without wing clipping. An interior Aviary can be a beautiful focal point with enough room to sit on a bench and bond with the birds directly. Provide dozens of perches and swings, some raised feeding areas, lots of bells, and safe toys. Your bird-pets will be very content. Naturalize with larger branches.

OUTDOOR BIRD AVIARIES

In the outdoors, a natural Aviary for wild birds can be created by planting a semi-circle of trees and shrubs for storm protection, with access to feeders, water, and suet. Put the Wild Bird Aviary in view of your favorite window and make sure the feeders are always full. Enjoy hours of enjoyment.

THE HEALING POWER OF BIRD SONG IN OUR LIVES

The sound of happy birds in the environment sends to our souls the message that "all is well." We are flooded with memories of sunshine, childhood, and gardening. In the depths of poverty, loneliness or depression, the sight of someone sitting on a park bench feeding the birds is a common sight. Why? Birds are like winged angelic messengers that do not pass judgment, and represent peace. In the Sisterhood of Healing Gardens birds are mystical messengers of light and hope.

Madonna of the Rose Garden

THE SPIRITUAL GARDEN OF THE MYSTICAL MADONNA

THE SPIRITUAL SYMBOLISM OF THE ROSE

Since ancient times, <u>roses</u> have symbolized God's hand at work. They are the masterpiece of the Creator, intricate and elegant. Their fragrance is spicy, complex yet delicate. Rose buds open, layer by layer, and represent the wisdom and spiritual path in people's lives. To many women, the Madonna, IS the ultimate Mystical Garden, a leader of the sacred path and Goddess of the Sisterhood.

When sending roses, each color has its own meaning:

- Red, the lover's rose, represents enduring passion
- White shows humility and innocence
- Yellow expresses sweet friendship and joy
- Pink offers gratitude, appreciation and admiration
- Orange represents enthusiasm and desire
- Lilac and purple roses represent enchantment and love at first sight.

Sisterhood

The Sarah- Moses

Rainbow Crones

CREATIVE MATRIARCHS

Sitting in a gift shop surrounded by displays of suitcases, purses, sculptures, and to my left a checkout counter, I had just punched my time card out at a bloody poultry processing line. I ran into the gift shop, cleaned up, changed into an antique black velvet dress, elbow high white gloves and seated myself at a small circular mosaic table.

The shop owner had placed white Lilies as a centerpiece in a clear glass vase. Here I was to read Tarot Cards and Palms for curious customers as they walked through the gift shop for a novel town night experience. Amongst the herbal aroma of vanilla and lavender, three women walked in the door with the jingle of a bell. Something was different about them. I felt as if they were white magic witches. A shiver went through me. Had my time come to be collected for a new threshold in time?

They were Rainbow Crone Matriarchs of significant purpose, it seemed. One woman, with a queenly stature, held the elbow of the second woman who gave me a charming smile with a searching anxiousness in her eyes. The third woman was child-like, poetic, and reminded me of an aging fairy.

I was an "Autumn", a sinking ship, sick to death of charismatic bad boys, performing music in a college pub filled with kids the age of my son. My fan audience went home to bed at 10:00 pm now. My side business, Psychic Readings, seemed destined to be my retirement job in a few years. The magical women walked towards me and introduced themselves. We spoke about the night, art, spirituality, and wouldn't I like to come to their area to read for a gathering. From that moment on, I became a chosen part of their Sisterhood, a circle of kindred souls with amazing gardens, unique personalities and singular artistic souls.

Beth and the Pine Tree Circle

GARDENS, FRIENDS AND TEA

The Sisterhood was sipping lemonade beneath the low hanging boughs of an evergreen tree. Thick Pine branches draped to the ground around us, as we sat within the inner sanctum of a perfect room. An ornate gate led to the center where a circle of wicker chairs awaited our ample rumps.

What truly added to the mystical hovel was that we were completely hidden just inches from the sidewalk. Evening walkers talked amongst themselves, and bicycles floated by while we sat hidden, a part of the tree. We were peaceful ghosts in a cemetery watching the world pass by. This was Beth's world, a sort of Roman Coliseum Spectator within the quiet essence of nature.

As the sun flickered through the branches, Beth explained the rules of Feng Shui directional garden placement. The mysterious feeling of peering through evergreen boughs, cascading crystals and fiber art suspended above us, was not a "typical" garden setting at all. In this tree-room, Beth was creative on her terms. Rules? We wanted to know these rules if we, too, were to create magical gardens. From our wicker circle, the voice of a respected area artist mumbled, "Hmmmph. Rules were made to be broken."

With a pause, Beth turned around and walked into the house, well aware her best friend had just rebelled against the very rules she based her gardens and art on. The trigger for her friend's anger was the word, "Feng Shui". Margaret lived her life, rebelliously. She created sculptures, Pagan garden masks, and gardens in honor of the elementals. It was her niche, and in all walks of life and religious faiths, the community loved and respected her.

Though Beth's circular Pine Room took our breath away with its magical other-worldliness, Margaret's garden was a backyard-stage-studio. In a circle, North, South, East, and West, four life-sized maiden sculptures stood, their heads tilted towards the sky. What were they looking for? Behind the maidens, a roughly built stage for performers. Simple white Daisies and ferns were sprinkled in the landscape. Like Beth, the significant placement of all elements was the direction of the energy they represented.

Village Wise Women –

THE WITCHES GARDEN

THE HEALING APOTHECARY OF THE MYSTICAL GARDEN

My first encounter with a witch was a neighbor that practised Pagan rituals privately within her home. The first time I saw her swinging a sword to the Cardinal directions, her long hair flowing, I was taken aback, and very curious. She was excited to share volumes of notebooks in which she collected Ancient knowledge, rituals, garden and herbal cures. On a wood bench in front of my studio she would share with great reverence the study of being a Witch. She was brilliant, college and formal military school educated. My stereotype of Witches and Pagans flew out the window.

THE WITCH GARDEN

Throughout time, villagers would travel to the outskirts of town to find the local witch for an herbal cure from her apothecary garden. As a Sarah Moses of healing these Village Wise Women had great knowledge of the five essential elements and how to combine compatible herbs for their magical elixirs from their gardens filled with herbs, vegetables, twigs, roots and vines. The five crucial culinary herbs in a witches garden are Rosemary, Basil, Mint, Sage, and Lemon Balm.

THE FIVE ELEMENTS OF THE MAGICAL HEALING GARDEN

The **Five Elements** of Nature and well-being are Earth, Water, Fire, Air, and Space. In the Mystical Healing Garden, symbolically represented with objects and shapes, each of these elements contribute to a fascinating and uplifting stroll through her mystical garden.

The Witch chooses her intention, but as a natural herbalist, the cures in her basket are often from her Apothecary garden or the woods. There is a knowledge of the Five Elements of Healing.

THE FIVE HERBAL ELEMENT IN THE BODY

Each element is responsible for different structures in the body.

- **Earth = bones, flesh, skin, tissues, and hair.** Earth's season is winter, and it's direction is North. In Nature it's environment is a cave, the symbol of shelter, the womb, rebirth, and the home of ancient oracles.
- **Water = saliva, urine, semen, blood, and sweat.** The energy of water is feminine and is symbolized by the womb. The Water Element affects the subconscious, emotions and dreams and is the element of love and emotions. It influences our moods and emotional responses. The energy of water rules the West and its season is Autumn. It heals and offers emotional release and removes all that is stagnant.
- **Fire = hunger, thirst, and sleep.** The fire element is associated with the sun, the giver of life, and governs passion, intensity, desire, intuition, understanding, imagination and possibilities. Fire cleanses and purifies. It is both creative and destructive.
- **Air = body movement, expansion, contraction, suppression.** Air governs the realm of the mind and all mental activity. Air's direction is east and its season is spring. It is the element of the wind and controls all movements associated with travel, freedom, thought, ideas, intellect, imagination and discovery. Space = physical attraction, repulsion, and fear.
- **Spirit = 7th Crown Chakra and akashic records, a record of all knowledge pertaining to the material planes and astral world.** Spirit is expressed through art, music, writing, religion, healing, magic.

If any element is impure or out of balance with another, disease and suffering may occur.

Are You a Sarah-Moses?

THE GENTLE WARRIOR

Many women of leadership reach a stage in their career where what they committed their entire life to no longer excites them. Just when they have reached a level of excellence, the challenge is gone. Accepting this reality in their life, their energy becomes distracted. Suddenly, from the side wings, young professional women, hungry for power, crowd in. This is the natural cycle of life and the survival of the species. Two choices are available. The Senior in charge, feeling threatened, can fight to hold her ground. The other option is to smile wisely, pass the baton, and mentor until she is confident her legacy is intact.

Some will go into shock once this happens, suddenly forced, with time on their hands, to see the things about themselves they were in denial of. But one day, eager to lead again, they will realize they have a second chance in life and new challenges are available. Public speaking, life coaching, writing, travel or becoming a facilitator of a Sisterhood enables leadership as a Gentle Warrior. Mentorship becomes the role of the Sarah Moses.

WHY IS SHE CALLED A SARAH MOSES?

In the Old Testament Sarah was nicknamed "the Mother of Nations" and conceived a child at 90 years old. Moses was a famous prophet who led his people across the Red Sea. Sarah-Moses is the name I have given a woman with the Yin-Yang ability to nurture and lead at the same time. In my Intuitive Work, I have spoken to many Sarah- Moses who find their calling.

It's important to remember to savor every moment now.

How to Lead in a Crisis

The Sarah– Moses as a Leader

When faced with a crisis, remember the fire drills at school. "Keep Calm and Walk." When faced with an unexpected crisis in your own life, at work, or in your city, how you act affects the attitude of everyone around you. As a Sarah- Moses, you are the compassionate Mother and Captain all in one.

LEADERSHIP TIPS

1} Take the Lead until Police or Higher Sources Take Charge – Do not be a part of group despair. Ask the hard questions. Listen to the answers and take action accordingly.

2} Stay Calm – If you have to channel the leader of your favorite disaster movie in order to maintain composure, be the part. Oprah Winfrey once said when you act the part of your favorite actor of empowerment at a job interview in order to stay composed, you will find it easier to be strong under fire.

3} Assemble Teams – Teams, depending on the crisis, will need the right people. One team will be needed for storm wreckage management, another for clean up. A team will check houses for survivors or wounded. Another team skilled at motivation can keep people uplifted and energized. Even the town drunk may find this is his time to shine.

4} Listen to the Facts – Gather all people with an important stake in the situation, then present and listen to the facts together. This makes good sense when contending with wounded egos.

5} Identify and Consider All Options – All solutions should be evaluated with pros and cons, cause and effect. Don't wait too long to take action. If you have a problem-solving team, hand this over to them.

6} Take a Walk to prevent overwhelming yourself.

The Reiki Rose

LONG DISTANCE HEALING FROM THE GARDEN

SENDING LONG DISTANCE HEALING

SENDING LOVE FROM THE HEALING GARDEN

There are times when we feel great concern for someone we love or care about. A pet has cancer, or we want to send healing to an area of the world where mass fire or an earthquake has ravaged the land. Sending the Reiki Rose to a specific person or place in a ball of pure illuminating light aids healing and transition. Placing our hands above our own body as a conduit, we empower the energy with the pure intention we send out.

STEPS FOR SENDING REIKI ROSE HEALING

1} In bed before you fall asleep, or in a quiet uninterrupted place, quiet your mind and take a deep breath

2} Envision your own body as a conduit of energy. At the same time envision the person, pet or place you want to send healing to. Say their name.

3} You may want to rub your hands together at this point, slowly bringing them together. The pulsing energy field you feel between them means you are ready, Place your hands above your body, sending the healing energy through you as a conduit, to the source.

4} Can you feel the electrical energy going out into the Universe? Send it as a rose or ball of light to the loved one you wish to heal. Five minutes or longer is enough.

5} Don't be upset if you fall asleep. In the deep state of making a connection, the Reiki Rose has been sent to heal.

6} Please remember that sending healing energy to those in hospice should be in the intention of helping them relax for a peaceful, loving transition.

How to Facilitate a Sisterhood Group

A Sisterhood Group is an intimate circle of women who inspire each other through chapters of life. Supportive of each other's goals, they are a shoulder to cry on when a crisis hits, or to ponder and share the good news and aspirations. For those alone, with or without children, a Sisterhood can replace family and be faithful rocks of support when needed, for funerals, childbirth, weddings, divorces, and aging. One does not need to have best friends in the sisterhood before coming together. An unspoken bond develops from being together. They are the friends you can pickup with at any time and know they will be welcoming. There are two Kinds of Sisterhood Groups; structured, and unstructured.

- A structured Sisterhood may have many members and need the order that rules, and a specific topic to consider in order that everyone stays focused.
- An unstructured Sisterhood may gather on specific days of the month, but always with new life stories and concerns that follow an impromptu format.

Tips for Facilitating a Sisterhood

- Create the right environment.... Will it be a home, cafe, public building?
- Ensure the expected objectives are clear...will there be food? New Members? Closed meetings?
- Establish expectations. ...Will political discussion be allowed? Will each meeting be at a different member's house? Will men be allowed?
- Energize the group bond throughout the meeting. ...What connects you? Recognize and respect differences without arguments. Allow time for thinking in silence, as well as offering new input if a lull in the conversation becomes awkward.
- Manage participation. ...will there be a talking stick to pass around for personal concerns. How long does each member get to talk?
- Adjust your facilitation style – Know when to lead, and when to back off, when to talk and when to listen.

I dedicate this book to Mom, who kneeled beside me and showed me the art of planting Zinnia seeds when I was a little girl and how to see the good in everyone. Thank you to my Sisterhood for the years of table talk bonding, dreams, sorrow and laughter.

Author's Biography

Ann Marie is a Mystic and member of a Sisterhood that has been together for over 11 years. Her first book series, "Gardens of the Sisterhood: Create a Mystical Garden," is her journey of reading land with Tarot, with colorful pictures of the magical gardens of her Sisterhood. Ann Marie's second book, "Gardens of the Sisterhood, Create a Mystical-Healing Garden," focuses on healing through the garden and its structure. The mystical principles of a Witch and Druid garden are discussed and how the Ancient elements of the garden are relevant in balancing a chaotic world. Ann Marie pays tribute to the Madonna and her Sacred leadership in Sisterhoods, with directions on how to facilitate a Sisterhood of one's own. As an Intuitive Reader and member of the new breed of Contemporary Alternative Healers, she defines the importance of blending into one's Community.

Printed in the United States
By Bookmasters